A Note to Parents and Teachers

DK READERS is a compelling programme for beginning readers, designed in conjunction with literacy experts, including Maureen Fernandes, B.Ed (Hons). Maureen has spent many years teaching literacy, both in the classroom and as a specialist in schools.

Beautiful illustrations and superb full-colour photographs combine with engaging, easy-to-read text to offer a fresh approach to each subject in the series.

Each DK READER is guaranteed to capture a child's interest while developing his or her reading skills, general knowledge and love of reading.

The five levels of DK READERS are aimed at different reading abilities, enabling you to choose the books that are exactly right for your child:

Pre-level 1: Learning to read
Level 1: Beginning to read
Level 2: Beginning to read alone
Level 3: Reading alone
Level 4: Proficient readers

The "normal" age at which a child begins to read can be anywhere from three to eight years old. Adult participation through the lower levels is very helpful for providing encouragement, discussing storylines and sounding out unfamiliar words.

No matter which level you select, you can be sure that y
child learn to rea

LONDON, NEW YORK, MUNICH,
MELBOURNE AND DELHI

For Dorling Kindersley
Designer Owen Bennett
Managing Art Editor Ron Stobbart
Managing Editor Catherine Saunders
Art Director Lisa Lanzarini
Publishing Manager Simon Beecroft
Category Publisher Alex Allan
Production Editor Sean Daly
Production Controller Rita Sinha
Reading Consultant Maureen Fernandes

For Lucasfilm
Executive Editor J. W. Rinzler
Editor Frank Parisi
Art Director Troy Alders
Keeper of the Indycron Leland Chee
Director of Publishing Carol Roeder

First published in Great Britain in 2011 by
Dorling Kindersley Limited,
80 Strand, London, WC2R 0RL

Copyright © 2011 Lucasfilm Ltd and ™
All rights reserved. Used under authorization.

Page design copyright © 2011 Dorling Kinderley Limited

2 4 6 8 10 9 7 5 3 1
176028—10/10

All rights reserved. No part of this publication may be
reproduced, stored in a retrieval system, or transmitted in any
form or by any means, electronic, mechanical, photocopying,
recording, or otherwise, without the prior written
permission of the copyright owner.

A CIP catalogue record for this book
is available from the British Library

ISBN 978-1-40534-735-8

Colour reproduction by Media Development and Printing Ltd, UK
Printed and bound in China by L.Rex

Discover more at

www.dk.com

www.indianajones.com

Contents

DK READERS

PROFICIENT READERS 4

INDIANA JONES

THE SEARCH FOR BURIED TREASURE

Written by W. Rathbone

Treasure hunter

The search for buried treasure is difficult and it can be dangerous. Fortunately, Indiana Jones has some special skills. Over the years he has found many legendary treasures including the Ark of the Covenant, the sacred Sankara Stones, the Holy Grail and an alien Crystal Skull.

Indy loves searching for rare artefacts. He also enjoys solving mysteries and travelling around the world. Indy has cut through deserts, jungles and rainforests. He has also explored castles, temples and secret tombs. However, he has learnt that sometimes the most civilized places can be the most dangerous.

Dr Jones
Indy's real name is Dr Henry Jones Jr. When he is not busy searching for treasure, he works as a professor of archaeology.

In an elegant Shanghai nightclub, Indy wears a stylish white suit, but has to evade death several times!

Dr Henry Jones
Indy inherited his name and also his love of history from his father, a professor of medieval literature.

Young explorer

Indy has always loved to explore, even from a young age. During a visit to Egypt, young Indy found his way into an old tomb. It was the tomb of Ka, an ancient king. In the tomb, Indy found his first buried treasure: the sculpted head of a jackal.

Now Indy is much older, but his love of searching for rare artefacts is as strong as ever. He continues his search for treasures whenever he can. Sometimes his son, Mutt, helps him out. Together Indy and Mutt travelled to Peru to look through an underground crypt for the mummy of a Spanish explorer.

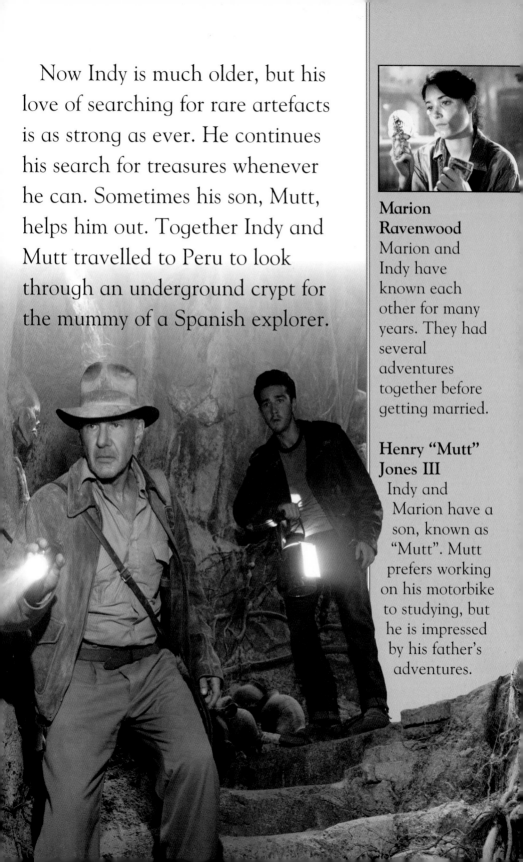

Marion Ravenwood
Marion and Indy have known each other for many years. They had several adventures together before getting married.

Henry "Mutt" Jones III
Indy and Marion have a son, known as "Mutt". Mutt prefers working on his motorbike to studying, but he is impressed by his father's adventures.

Humpy ride
On a trip to the
deserts of Egypt,
young Indy
learnt how to
ride a camel.

8

Along for the ride

The quest for exotic treasures often takes Indy to remote places where there are no proper roads or any modern forms of transportation. Indy has had to learn how to get around on all kinds of animals.

Indy and his friends were given elephants to ride when on the trail of the Sankara Stones in India. The elephants had a peculiar odour. Indy was not bothered by the smell, but his friend Willie did not like it. She poured a whole bottle of perfume over her elephant to make it smell nicer!

On horseback
As a Boy Scout, Indy enjoyed a lot of horse riding and got a taste of adventure.

Willie Scott
Wilhelmina "Willie" Scott is a nightclub singer who first met Indiana Jones in Shanghai.

On the road in India, Indy rides an elephant in search of the Sankara Stones.

9

*Indy tells Short
Round and Willie to
hold on for dear life!*

Family trip
In Peru, Marion
drove while
Mutt watched
his dad
eliminate traffic
in front of them
– with a
bazooka!

Transport tales

Indiana Jones often travels great
distances. Over the years he has had
to drive, pilot or just hang on to a
variety of vehicles. Sometimes Indy
needs to get somewhere in a hurry,
but other times he needs to make a
fast getaway using whatever vehicle
he can find. To escape
the Temple of Doom, he
jumped into a mine car
with his friends Willie
and Short Round.

During another getaway Indy stole a motorbike – and his dad rode in the sidecar. Nazis were chasing them so Indy wanted to get far away. However, Indy's father wanted them to go to the Nazi headquarters in Berlin!

Henry knew that he would find his diary there and that it would lead them to the priceless Holy Grail.

Air adventure
The Jones' journey from Berlin involved a biplane, with Indy's dad in charge of the machine gun.

Indy and his father do not always agree on everything.

Father always knows best
Indy might have been steering the motorbike, but Henry told his son which way to go – straight to their enemies' headquarters.

Holiday reading
Young Indy took books to read while on a trip in Kenya, Africa.

Read all about it

Indiana Jones has always loved to read, especially history books. He knows many things about ancient cultures and civilizations. This knowledge is very useful when he is hunting for rare artefacts.

Young Indy reads with his friend Meto of the Kenyan Massai tribe.

Ark of the Covenant
The Ark is where the prophet Moses is believed to have placed the list of ancient biblical rules known as the Ten Commandments.

Indy enjoys teaching others about history.

Indy has also mastered many languages, including Latin and Sanskrit, to help him in his search for elusive treasures. His knowledge of ancient texts helped him to find the sacred Ark of the Covenant before anyone else.

Ark book
This illustration shows the power of the Ark. It could destroy whole armies!

Patient teacher
During his early travels, Indy was taught by his patient and wise tutor, Helen.

Young explorer
In India, Indy encountered a young philosopher named Krishnamurti.

Far and wide

The search for buried treasure takes Indiana Jones all over the globe. He tours many countries and cities, visiting temples, churches and monuments. One adventure in India lead Indy to a hidden temple where he had to do battle with an evil priest to uncover the Sankara Stones.

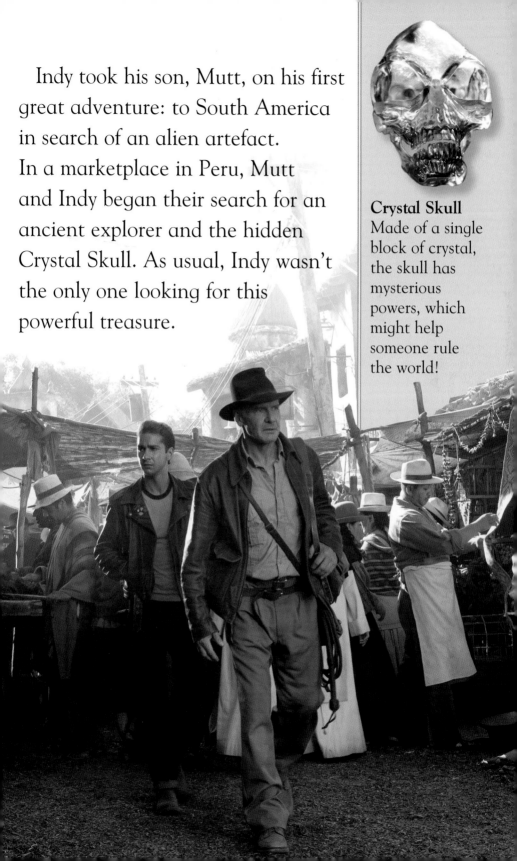

Indy took his son, Mutt, on his first great adventure: to South America in search of an alien artefact. In a marketplace in Peru, Mutt and Indy began their search for an ancient explorer and the hidden Crystal Skull. As usual, Indy wasn't the only one looking for this powerful treasure.

Crystal Skull
Made of a single block of crystal, the skull has mysterious powers, which might help someone rule the world!

Abner Ravenwood
Marion Ravenwood's father, Abner, devoted his life to studying texts and objects relating to the Ark of the Covenant.

When Indy was hunting for the Ark of the Covenant, his quest took him to a desolate snowy mountain in Nepal, Asia. He was determined to find the sacred treasure before the Nazis and believed that his old teacher Abner Ravenwood could help him.

The Nazis hoped that the power of the Ark would help them destroy their enemies, but Indy wasn't about to let that happen!

Indy hoped to find a clue that would lead him to the Ark – the headpiece of Ra. In a tiny village tavern he found his old friend Marion Ravenwood. Indy learnt that Marion's father was dead. Unfortunately some Nazi thugs also arrived, determined to fight Indy for the headpiece. During their struggle, a fire was started and the tavern burned down. The Nazis fled but Indy escaped with the headpiece.

Nazis
Arnold Toht was a Nazi agent.
The Nazis were the ruling party of Germany between 1933 and 1945.

Close call
Indy is nearly choked, shot and set on fire. However, thanks to his quick thinking – and a little help from Marion – Indy survives.

Indy must use his brain as well as his strength to outsmart the Nazi thugs.

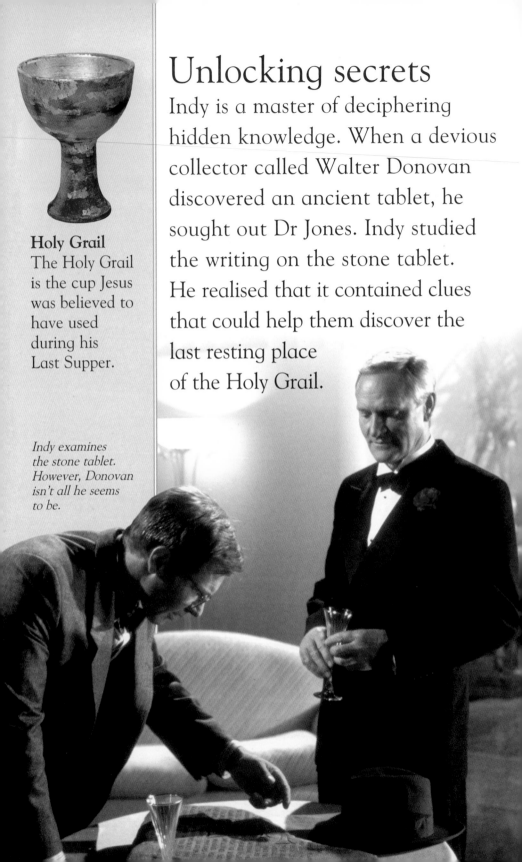

Unlocking secrets

Indy is a master of deciphering hidden knowledge. When a devious collector called Walter Donovan discovered an ancient tablet, he sought out Dr Jones. Indy studied the writing on the stone tablet. He realised that it contained clues that could help them discover the last resting place of the Holy Grail.

Holy Grail
The Holy Grail is the cup Jesus was believed to have used during his Last Supper.

Indy examines the stone tablet. However, Donovan isn't all he seems to be.

However, sometimes even Dr Jones needs help to understand ancient clues. During his quest to find the Ark, Indy needed help from an expert astrologer to decode the ancient markings of the headpiece of Ra. The wise man was able to tell Indy the correct height for the staff on which he should place the headpiece to help him find the Ark.

Headpiece of Ra
The fabulous headpiece is adorned with mysterious symbols and writings on both sides. Only an expert can decipher its clues.

Finding clues

Whether sneaking through perilous jungles or carefully searching dusty libraries, Indy has to decipher many different clues and signs. Sometimes important clues will be incomplete or damaged.

When Indy was looking for treasure hidden in an ancient temple, he found half of an old map. He bargained with a colleague to get the second half and then used his skills to find the treasure.

Maps
Many maps are incredibly detailed, but Indy often has to rely on extremely simple or ancient maps made by amateurs: is that a path or a dangerous cliff?

Sometimes clues are carefully hidden, but other times they might be staring Indy in the face. In an old library in Italy, Indy was looking for the entrance to an even older crypt. Here, "X" marked the spot. Indy found the secret world beneath the library, although he had to break through the floor without alerting the librarian! Far below, among the crumbling skeletons, Indy hoped to find another clue leading to the Holy Grail.

Crypt
Crypts are hidden chambers, usually underground. Indy found a marker in a crypt pointing toward the Holy Grail.

Longtime enemy
René Belloq is a rival archaeologist who cares only for money and power.

Arab dress
Most Arab countries are hot, so people must wear loose clothes to keep them cool. Indy's flowing robes and headdress also made a great disguise!

Treasure rivals

The search for treasure can often lead Indy straight into danger. That is because his enemies are searching for the same thing – and they will stop at nothing to get it. It is often a race against time between Indy and the bad guys. Because he is resourceful and never gives up, Indy usually wins.

During the hunt for the Ark of the Covenant, Indy disguised himself as an Arab tribesman to avoid being caught by Nazis. Then he used a rope to descend into a concealed Map Room without anyone noticing him.

In the Map Room, Indy placed the headpiece of Ra on a precisely measured staff. Clever Indy was now one step ahead of the Nazis!

Hieroglyphics
The walls of the Map Room are covered in an ancient Egyptian language that used pictures known as hieroglyphics to convey words.

Found it!
When sunlight shone through the headpiece, it magically illuminated the chamber where the Ark of the Covenant lay hidden.

Watch out!

Precious artefacts are often heavily guarded. Sometimes they are protected by deadly traps and snares, other times they are patrolled by fearsome animals. Indy is not frightened of nasty snares or dangerous booby traps, but there is one thing he is terrified of – snakes.

No fear
Young Indy had no fear of snakes. When his friend was frightened by a snake, Indy grabbed the creature and tossed it aside.

New fear
Indy developed a phobia after falling into a crate of snakes. Since then he has really hated them.

On his quest for the Sankara Stones in the Temple of Doom Indy came face to face with a snake. Was it real or a statue? Indy looked away and when he turned back, the mysterious snake had vanished into thin air!

Rats!

Indy's father does not have a problem with snakes, but he does hate rats. When Indy encountered hundreds of rats in a crypt, he remarked that his dad would have been scared to death!

Sankara Stones
Legend says there are five sacred stones. When they are close to each other, the diamonds within glow mysteriously.

Chilled monkey brains
Willie had been really looking forward to dinner.
She declined the bugs and when offered brains instead, she fainted.

Strong personality

Sometimes Indy needs a strong arm and an even stronger stomach to seek out precious treasure.

The search for the buried Sankara Stones led Indiana and his friends Willie and Short Round to Pankot Palace. It seemed like a very civilized place. Indy met royalty, ministers, officers, rich guests – and ate very scary food. When Indy and Willie attended a great banquet they were served boiled black beetles, eyeball soup and python, poached and stuffed with live baby eels!

After dinner, things got worse for Indy. He returned to his room and was attacked, and he soon discovered that children were being used to dig for the Sankara Stones. Indy was determined to save them, but first he had to face the guardians of a sinister temple: the Thuggees!

Thuggees
The Temple of Doom was controlled by a group known as Thuggees who worshipped the goddess Kali.

Best friend
During his adventures as a young man, Indy often needed help from his good friend Rémy.

Short Round
Indy found the orphan Short Round in Shanghai. He turned out to be a very good pal, and helped Indy escape from a gambling club.

Helping hand

Even Indiana Jones sometimes needs a helping hand. In fact, Indy needs all the friends he can get during his many perilous adventures! Some of Indy's friends are loyal, but some of them are not so loyal.

In the jungles of India, Indy and his friend Short Round cheated each other at cards. But when it counted, Short Round saved Dr Jones's life.

Walter Donovan, however, only pretended to be Indy's friend. He wanted the Holy Grail at any cost and used Indy's skills to find it. Then Donovan turned his guns on the adventurer and claimed his prize.

Sallah
Sallah has gone
on many
adventures with
Indy. He lives
in Cairo and
helped his friend
dig up the
Ark of the
Covenant.

Elsa
Dr Elsa
Schneider is a
double agent.
She is willing
to help Indy as
long as his
work benefits
her – and
her Nazi
employers.

Although his friends have often
saved his life, Indy has also come to
the rescue of his pals many times.
He was not sure if Elsa Schneider
was his friend or enemy, but when
she was threatened by a Nazi he
preferred not to take any chances.

*Indy is beginning to
wish that he hadn't
trusted Elsa Schneider.*

His father told Indy that Elsa was a Nazi, but Indy was torn. He threw down his gun so that Elsa would not be harmed but in the next instant he realised his mistake. She was a Nazi! Indy learnt the hard way that he should have listened to his father.

Marcus Brody
Marcus is a friend to both Indy and his father. He runs a museum and sends Indy on many missions to retrieve ancient objects.

George "Mac" McHale
Mac is also a double agent. When he is in debt, he will work for anyone, even if it means harming his friend Indy.

Golden idol
The ancient Chachapoyans created a golden fertility idol. Many explorers had met their death trying to acquire it.

Treasure dangers!

The best part of searching for hidden treasures is the thrill of discovery. This exciting moment, however, often is extremely dangerous – treasure does not always want to be found!

When Indy finally located a golden idol in an ancient temple, he slowly reached out to collect his prize.

The idol sits on a pressure-sensitive disk. If the idol is taken, deadly traps are sprung!

However, by lifting the idol, Indy set off many traps. Firstly he had to avoid poison darts, then he had to leap over a bottomless chasm. Next his friend betrayed him and then an enormous boulder came crashing toward him! Finally, Indy threw himself headlong through spider webs into the jungle outside. Unfortunately, Belloq was waiting there to take the idol. Better luck next time, Indy!

Treasure thief
Belloq used members of the Hovito tribe to help him retrieve the idol from Indy.

More snakes
Indy was less than pleased to see the floor appear to be writhing. It was covered in thousands of pythons and cobras!

Indy uses surveying tools like transits and levels to pinpoint the Ark's location.

The search for the Ark was also extremely dangerous. It took Indy to North Africa, where he located the area under which the valuable artefact lay. His enemies slept all around him, but Indy told his men to start digging in the desert sand. The sky turned dark and lightning split the clouds. It seemed as if nature itself was angry!

After digging through the night, Indy descended through an opening to find the powerful buried treasure.

Buried alive
Cruel Gestapo agent Toht pushed Marion into the antique tomb and sealed her in with Indy. He hoped they enjoyed their living death!

Jackal god
Indy had to climb an enormous statue of a jackal to escape and pursue the Ark, which was taken by the Nazis.

True test
Indy had to avoid deadly traps on his way to the Grail room. At one point, huge circular blades threatened to cut him in two!

Faith
Indy had to summon all of his faith to take a step into what looked like a bottomless chasm.

On another occasion, Indy discovered the last resting place of the Holy Grail, but found more than one cup. He had to use all of his learning and instincts to work out which cup was the true Grail.

Choosing the wrong cup would result in a horrible death. Fortunately, Indy remembered that Jesus was a modest man so he would not have used a jewel-encrusted vessel.

Wrong cup
Donovan followed Indy to the Grail room and chose poorly. The result? Instant aging into dust!

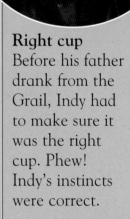

Right cup
Before his father drank from the Grail, Indy had to make sure it was the right cup. Phew! Indy's instincts were correct.

Grail knight
The bravest Crusader was one of three brothers who had sworn to protect the Holy Grail.

Hidden treasure

The word "treasure" can mean many things. It can be a valuable idol or a precious relic, but it can also mean something, or someone, much closer to home. Finding the Grail cup meant that once again Indy had triumphed over his enemies, and it also made him realise how much he loved his father.

When the wicked Donovan shot Henry, Indy had to enter the Grail sanctuary to save his father.

The Grail knight greets Indy after guarding the Grail for 700 years.

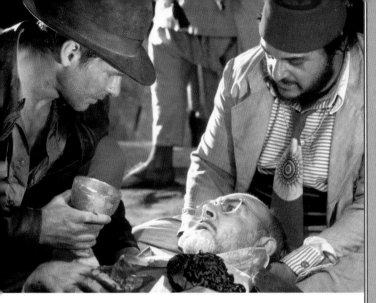

Bad Elsa
Elsa couldn't resist the promise of immortality so she grabbed the Grail and ran for the exit.

After finding the true Grail cup, Indy poured water from it into his father's wound. Miraculously it healed almost instantly. Henry felt as good as new, which was a good thing because Elsa was about to make a dangerous mistake!

Grail diary
Thanks to his father's detailed diary, Indy was able to locate the Holy Grail.

Wise father
Henry Sr knew that the cave would collapse if anyone walked over the floor's Great Seal with the Grail.

Some treasures are just not meant to be kept. When Elsa Schneider tried to take the Holy Grail out of the cave, she triggered an earthquake. Indy tried to save her, but Elsa's desire for the Grail was too great and she fell into a chasm.

The Grail lay perched on a ledge almost within reach, so Indy tried to grab it. He stretched with all his might but the earthquake was reducing the cave to rubble. Indy wisely chose to save his own life, rather than recapture the Grail.

Compassion
Indy was willing to forgive Elsa for trying to kill him but Elsa was determined to get the Grail so she let go of Indy's hand.

On the run
His strength returned, Henry was led out of the cave by Indy to their waiting horses. They then rode into the sunset.

Precious treasure

Finding rare artefacts can be just the beginning of the story. What happens afterwards can be almost as much of an adventure! Indiana Jones believes that most treasures should be kept safe, and that, in most cases, the best place for them is in a museum.

As a young man, Indy resolved to return the Cross of Coronado to a museum. It took him many years to do so, but he eventually succeeded.

Cross of Coronado
While on a Boy Scout outing, Indy discovered grave robbers just as they unearthed a fabled golden crucifix.

After Indy found the three Sankara Stones, he knew that he had to do the right thing. Although two were lost in his final battle with an evil priest, he returned one of them to its village home. Without the stone, the people were starving and ragged, but with the return of the sacred stone and their children the people thrived once again.

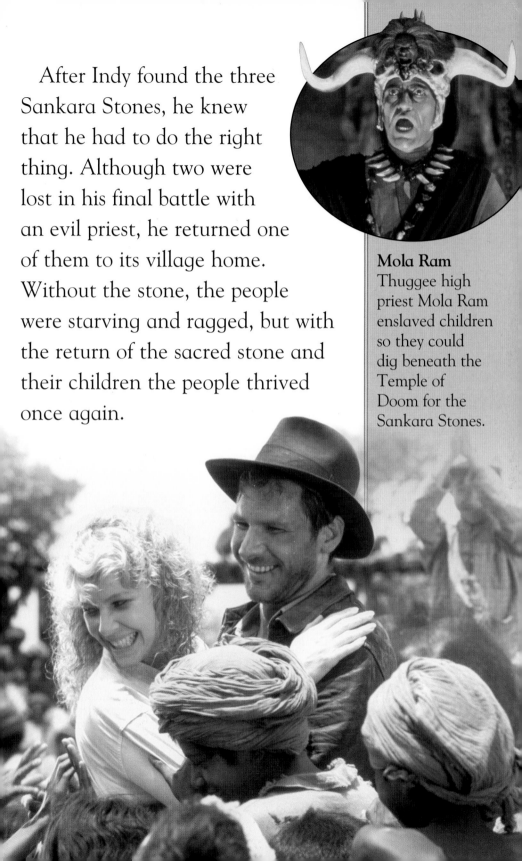

Mola Ram
Thuggee high priest Mola Ram enslaved children so they could dig beneath the Temple of Doom for the Sankara Stones.

Beyond treasure

The adventures of Indiana Jones could fill a whole library. However, Indy is more than just a great teacher and a brave treasure hunter. During World War I, young Indy joined the Belgian army to fight against Germany and its allies. The horrible warfare in the trenches was his most terrifying ordeal.

Indy also fought in World War II. He was a soldier and an intelligence agent, working against the Nazis and their allies. After that, Indy was involved in the Cold War. When the Russians pursued the Crystal Skull, Indy leaped into action to find it first. After all, finding treasure is what Indiana Jones does best.

World War II
Between 1939 and 1945 World War II was fought between the Axis powers, which included Germany, Japan and Italy, and the Allies, which included Britain, France and the United States of America.

The Cold War
After World War II relations were tense between Communist countries in the East, such as the Soviet Union, and countries in the West, such as the USA.

Secret treasure

Some treasures are too dangerous to be displayed in a museum. Although Indy travelled around the world and risked his life several times to obtain the Ark of the Covenant, no one would ever know about it.

Souvenirs
Indy's classroom contains many mementos of his adventures, including a sacred mask and an ancient carving.

Area 51
Rumour has it that the Ark is stored in the infamous Area 51, a top secret US military base in Nevada.

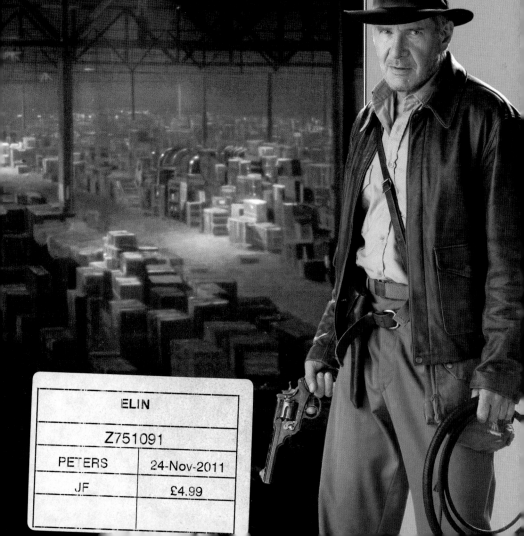

Some mysterious yet powerful people decided that the Ark must be hidden. So it was sealed in a crate and stored in a gigantic warehouse. Its location remains a closely guarded secret, known only to a few people.

Further adventures
In his trademark fedora, Indy has become a legend – but for him life is the greatest adventure!

Glossary

Allies
People on the same side in a war.

Archaeology
The study of ancient life and objects.

Artefacts
Man-made objects, often from the past.

Bazooka
A hand-held weapon that can fire rockets.

Booby trap
An explosive device that is set off when a harmless-looking object is touched.

Chasm
A deep crack in the ground.

Civilized
A society that has developed culturally.

Communist
A country whose government controls everything that is produced so that everyone has equal wealth.

Decipher
To work out the meaning of something.

Double agent
A spy who pretends to work for one government but works for another.

Elusive
Difficult to find.

Fedora
A soft felt hat.

Idol
A statue that is worshipped as a god.

Immortality
The ability to live forever.

Intelligence agent
A spy who collects information about an enemy.

Jackal
An animal that is similar to a dog.

Mementos
Objects kept to remember an event.

Mummy
A dead body that is wrapped in cloth before it is buried.

Perilous
With a risk of great danger.

Phobia
A great fear of something.

Relic
A precious part of something old that has remained.